How to manage your e-reputation

Collection: 50 minutes to control

Pierre CAT

On Off Line

Editions

This book is from the platform www.pierrecat.com.
"Pierre CAT" and "pierrecat. com" are registered trademarks of Pierre Cat Consulting sarl.
Publisher: On Off Line sprl
Avenue Louise 523
1050 Brussels
Phone: +32 2 880 80 88
ISBN: 978-2-39035-002-6
Release date: December 2017

Illustrations: by the author and fromPixabay (sous licence CC0
(Creative Commons Zero)).

ISBN

9 782390 350026

Table of contents

What is e-reputation?

Digital identity and e-reputation are important topics for any Internet user.

They represent the two sides of the same coin: your digital identity (what we know about you) and your e-reputation (what we say about you) are closely linked.

Today, a large majority of Internet users are now asking about the people they will meet in real life: job seekers, prospects, new customers, future partners, future suppliers...

Professional digital identity

The professional digital identity and everything I say, do, publish, both professionally and personally on the Internet. So the traces that we leave on line through our profiles, publications, comments and other activities have an impact on the opinion that people will be able to make about us.

Be inspired by Warren Buffett's sentence:

"It takes 20 years to build a reputation and five minutes to ruin it."

More worryingly, we can distinguish two types of traces left on Google or social networks: those that we have produced and those that we are not aware of. The latter can also be even more dangerous.

From private to professional

A study by Gallup (1) reveals that 94% of users of social networks connect to friends and family. And think that they have no role in their professional life.

Moreover, a new study conducted by Norton (2) shows that even Internet users between the ages of 18 and 34, who were born with social networks and the Internet, are not aware of the importance of their digital life.

In this study, 3,038 French, British and Germans were interviewed.

26 to 31% (depending on the countries concerned) of 18-34 year olds are not aware of the results of a search for their name. Unpleasant surprises are common, with 14% stunned by the results:

- 32% discover an old social network profile
- 33% discover a profile they thought they were not accessible
- 27% were surprised to see content published without their permission
- 18% were surprised to appear in some photos or videos

A challenge for everyone

Taking care of your digital identity is a key issue for job seekers as most recruiters scan the Internet for information about job seekers. But it is also important for current employees. Because more and more jobs have a digital dimension and it is obvious that managing your online reputation is a necessary skill for a large number of employees.

Business leaders, managers and sales people are also closely concerned by their digital identity and e-reputation, which will be scrutinised by all their business contacts.

We will see in this book how to manage its digital identity and improve its e-reputation.

Online reputation is increasingly important for finding a job

Today, online reputation is very important for finding a job or an internship.

Recruitment

Recruiters almost systematically use the Internet to search for profiles via social networks or directly on Google.
Digital information is therefore increasingly important to identify the right profiles (and conversely, to be identified).

The e-reputation of candidates

In the U. S., more and more companies are requiring recent graduates to have a Klout score (see below) of more than 35 in their recruitment.

E-reputation therefore strongly influences employability.

The situation is not yet the same in Europe, but similar requirements are beginning to be put in place.

A word of advice: don't underestimate this factor!

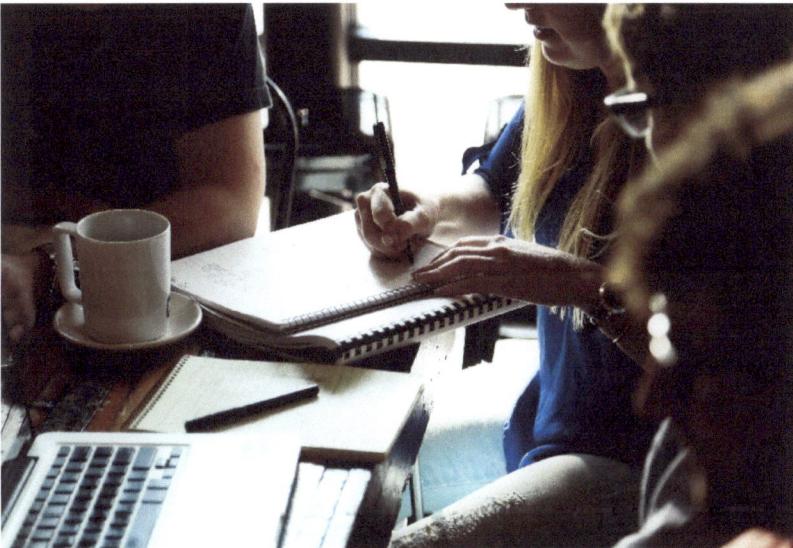

The opportunity to stand out

While the importance of the content published on the web and social networks is no longer to be proved, their significance is not necessarily negative, quite the contrary.

Building and improving your professional digital identity can be a real opportunity.

You can differentiate yourself and reveal your personality through your profile, attract and reassure recruiters or your future boss.

Anything the recruiter perceives of your personality will potentially make him or her want to meet you or favour your application over another candidate with a similar profile.

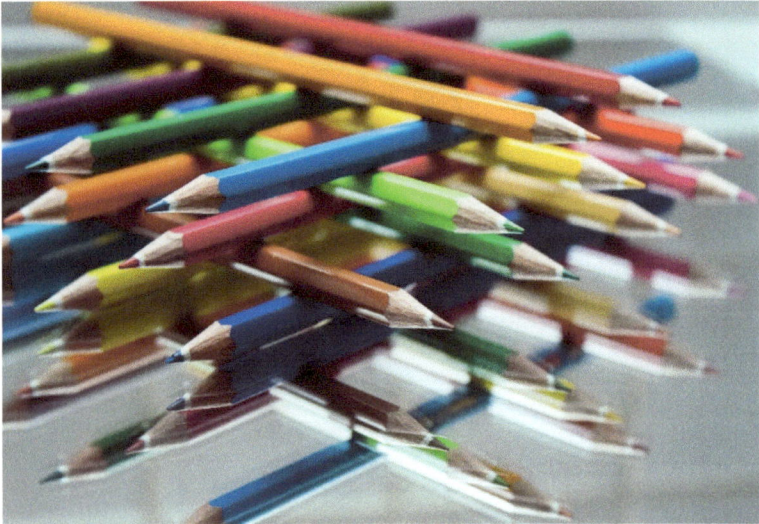

The importance of e-reputation for employees

Taking care of your digital identity is a key issue for current employees.

To stand out from the crowd

Cultivating your e-reputation can also allow employees to be exposed to new opportunities.

It is not because we work in companies that we are, on the one hand, secure in the face of criteria for "corporate reorganisation" and, on the other hand, that we are no longer "on the market" for access to potential promotions or internal transfers.

The important thing is to be noticed, to convey a positive image and demonstrate your mastery of digital communication.

In addition, companies appreciate the fact that their employees become " ambassadors ", i. e. they convey and support the company's culture and values.

Your external image can thus allow you to progress and transmit a good image internally. And, why not, also attract external proposals...

Developing your Network

Taking care of your digital image is a way to expand your network and make new contacts. Your visibility, the quality of your publications or comments, will allow you to be "followed" by other professionals and integrate into different communities.
This will make it easier for you to be notified early of vacancies or other opportunities.

Improve your strategic foresight

This presence in different communities will also allow you to confront your problems with your colleagues, to share ideas, to compare the results obtained (of course, without breaking any obligation of confidentiality!...).
This sharing of experience, as well as easy access to a set of information, will allow you to be more efficient on a daily basis and be able to prove to your superiors that you are aware of the latest developments in your sector.

CEO, executives and salespeople, wake up!

Up to the highest echelons

While digital identity and e-reputation are important for jobseekers and employees, they are vital for employers, managers and salespeople.

If they are in contact with customers, prospects and suppliers, these values will be examined or likely to be examined at any time.

Moreover, if the commercial stakes are high, their e-reputation will be scrutinised by their interlocutors. Because it is inconceivable, at the moment, to do business with a company and managers who do not have a good e-reputation!

The company on the front line

A phenomenon in full explosion, the reputation of a company is judged as such, but also on the sum of the value of the e-reputation of each of its managers.

This is why more and more companies are requiring their managers to have at least a complete and, if possible, particularly active LinkedIn profile.

The quality of the content published by its staff will benefit the company as a whole.

At the same time, any questionable action by one of its members may be prejudicial to it.

The importance of a charter

The company thus exposed and vulnerable to the potential actions of its employees must imperatively set up a charter for the use of social networks.

They give advice and guidance to their employees to force good practices.

For if they are informed of what it is better to do and what should never be done, then they will not be able to play the card "I didn't know me, sir".

Moreover, the stakes of productivity, confidentiality, respect for the company and people are not trivial concerns.

Some employers go so far as to include these obligations in employment contracts.

While this practice is tending to spread, a study by Robert Half shows that 53% of the private companies surveyed have not yet implemented a charter or contractual regulation governing the private use of social networks by their employees.

Set up a monitoring service

In order to avoid harmful behaviour, anticipate problems and tensions, detect risk factors, a vigilance service must be set up! Some people call it e-Reputation Watch.

This vigilance can concern employees, but also the media, suppliers and customers.

Positive, but above all negative opinions cannot be taken lightly and must be followed up.

Monitoring tools such as "Mention" can be of great help. Or, at least,"Google Alerts"!

Let's draw up a battle plan!

Now that you've understood the importance of digital identity and e-reputation, it's time to put a battle plan in place.

I propose a five-step process:

Step 1: Sensitise yourself through self-investigation!
Step 2: Correct what can be corrected!
Step 3: Refine your professional identity!
Step 4: Exist digitally!
Step 5: Get under control!

Step 1: Sensitise yourself by investigating yourself!

It is important to take stock when we are questioning our professional digital identity.

Because a young graduate has, in principle, a less developed digital identity than a confirmed professional. The latter must therefore build its digital identity or transform a private identity into a professional digital identity.

On the other hand, a confirmed professional will have to consolidate his digital identity or, if it contains clumsiness or flaws, modify it.

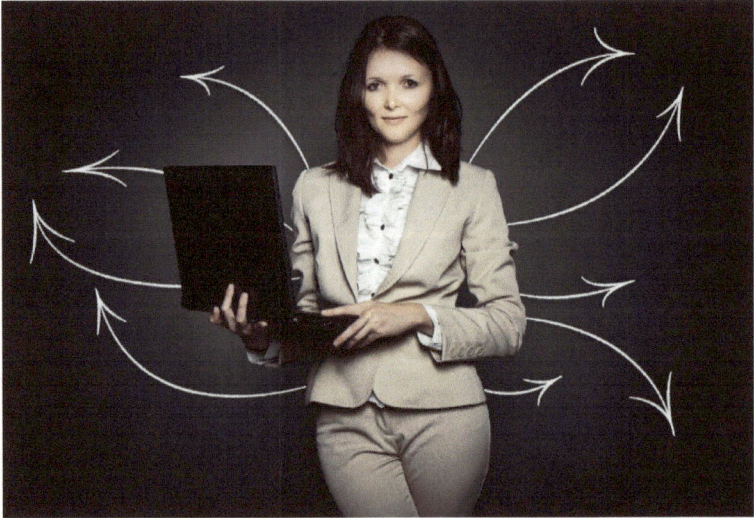

If digital traces exist, the content of these traces should be assessed.
Are there any negative traces attached to my name or business? If that is the case, we have to deal with this information and filter out the information that is harmful to us from that which highlights us.

Let's look together at how we can do this investigation and find out who we seem to be in the eyes of those who want to know more about us.

Traditional search engines : Google

To test your digital identity, the basic search must be done on Google, it is the reference search engine for many Internet users.

Indeed, by typing your name, or the name of the person you are looking for, you can via Google find the information the search engine has in its database.

This information will relate to the person's site, if it has one and if it is well referenced, the mention of his name on other sites, as well as his presence on the main social networks.

... and Bing

You can also do the same operation on other search engines like Bing (Microsoft) to check if the results are the same.

You will notice in both slides that the sites listed under my name are not exactly the same and the images are different as well.

It should be noted that in both cases the pictures of cats are not linked to my account, neither professional nor private.

The test on social networks

If you are researching yourself, you should know what social networks you are present on and how.

On the other hand, if you do it for another person, you can search directly on the different social networks for the name of the person you are interested in.

In fact, most social networks make available an internal search engine that makes it possible to find both the person you are looking for and also mentions of the name of the person that can be made in the posts, as is the case, for example, on Twitter.

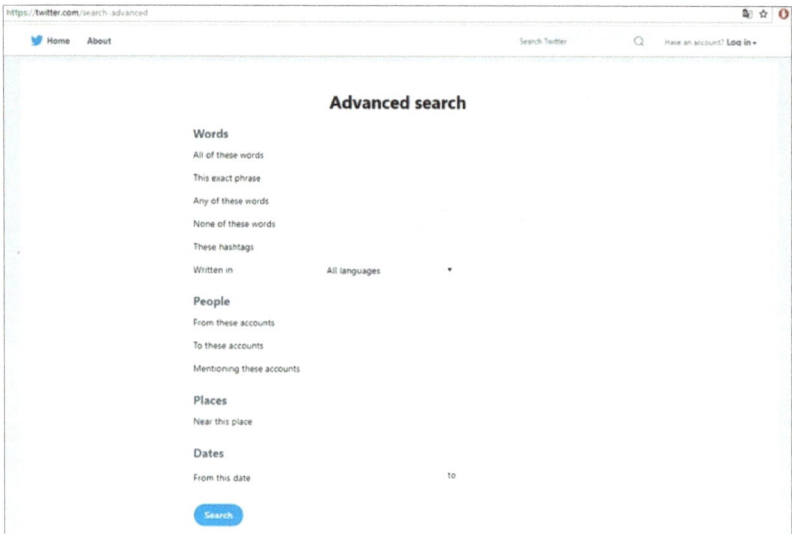

Specific tools (web and social networks)

If you don't want to search manually, specialised sites can do it for you.

The most famous and oldest, Pipl (www.pipl.com) allows you to have a complete scan of a whole set of information at the level of websites and social networks, but also other information such as telephone information, for example.

The site is quite well done and even if it is free, it can offer you a certain precision, because it makes a search in two steps. First, the search is done on your name and the site displays a list of profiles with a portrait. As soon as you have chosen one of the profiles offered, it carries out a complete analysis of the information available to it.

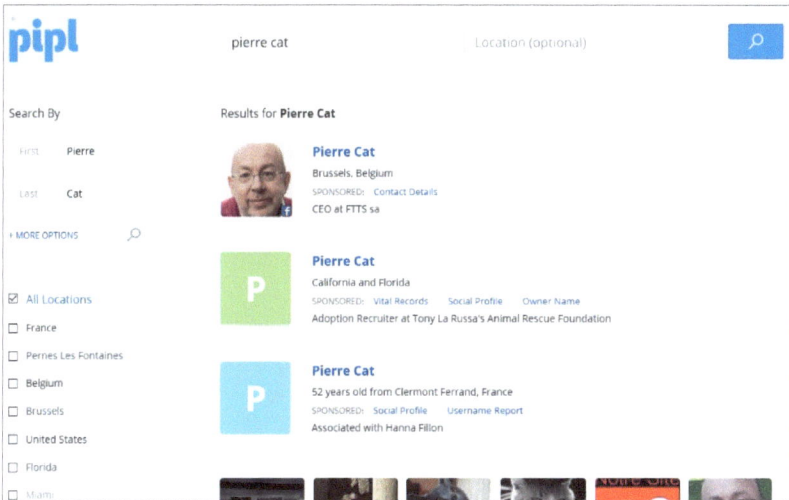

Alternatives to Pipl

Other websites like People Explorer (www.peoplexplorer.com) and Owler (www.owler.com) also allow you to search by name and location.

Find hidden accounts

If you think you have forgotten a social network subscription or if you are looking for someone else's social networks and you think they may have hidden profiles, the Namecheck site (www.namechk.com) can be interesting in your search.

Its operation is very simple, just enter the username that you think is relevant and the site will search if it is available on social networks (this also works with domain names). If it is no longer available, you can always check if the account opened with this username belongs to the person you are looking for.

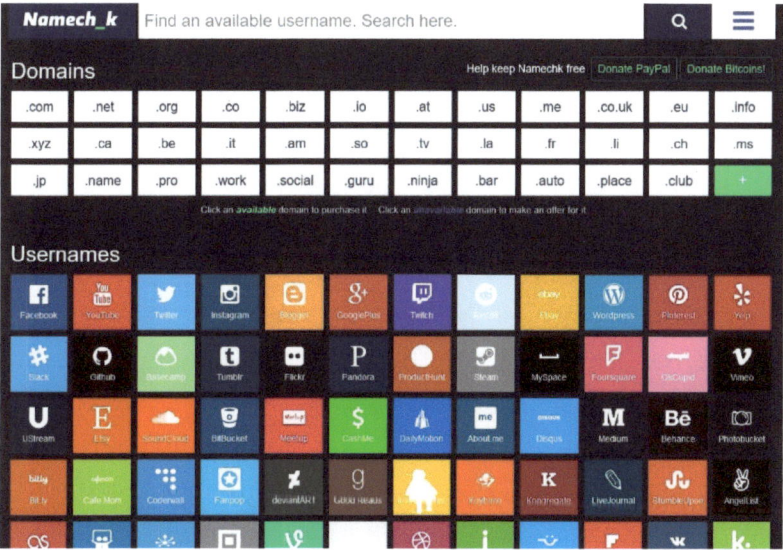

Naturally, this service has not been created for this purpose since it allows you to determine in principle whether your user name is still available to reserve a domain name or open an account on a social network...

Activity scores

Several sites allow you to test your activity score on the main social networks.

It is not a question of testing here your e-reputation, these tools are basic.

They analyse the number of accounts opened, your regularity of publication, the number of your subscribers, etc.

There are many, but here are three free tools that can help you more or less efficiently in this analysis:
- Webmii (www.webmii.com)
- and the most famous, Klout (www.klout.com)

Webmii

In the case of the Webmii website (www.webmii.com) which offers you to test your presence on social networks for free and give you a score.

I ran a test on my name.

On the one hand, I notice that my score is low. It is true that I am not very active at the moment on social networks...

This score is, of course, to be taken with great care since it is only a summary and free analysis of your activity at any given time. So don't block on this number, it doesn't represent something very reliable as it is, just an indication.

But in my case, it's a "reminder" to be active again on my social networks...

On the other hand, the pictures that are taken again are not linked at all to my accounts on social networks or other platforms. In fact, all the images, except the two portraits of myself, are not at all relevant.

This may sound anecdotal, but it does call into question the attribution of the collected data (problem of homonymy) and thus the reliability of the result.

Klout

The best known is Klout (www.klout.com) which also gives you a visibility score.

The analysis is more comprehensive and professional because you must allow Klout to have access to your various social networks and Klout will be able, in detail, to test your presence, visibility and notoriety on the different social networks.

As I have already mentioned, some companies ask their employees or future employees to have a minimum Klout score, to ensure that they have a real presence on social networks and a real visibility.

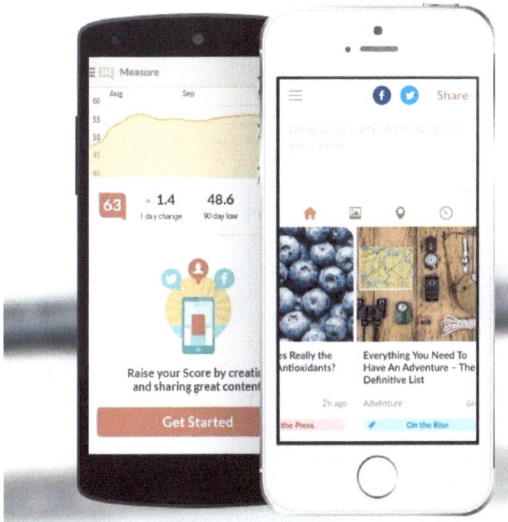

Corporate tools

If you want to check if a person is an administrator of a company, you can check it through this site: OpenCorporates. com. It allows you to know if a person is present in a company worldwide and so the search can be very detailed.

opencorporates •••••

The largest open database of companies in the world

| Search 138,048,504 companies | All jurisdictions ▾ | Q |

◉ Companies ◯ Officers   Browse all jurisdictions

Winner Open Data Business Award 2015

The e-reputations tools

There are a lot of tools on the market because it represents a huge challenge at the professional level. It will be difficult in the context of this book, to detail all the tools that exist. I'll give you the best-known ones.

All these tools are paid for and, of course, are more relevant and professional than the free tools.

These tools make a much more in-depth analysis of your data and also offer access to a database that they have built up over time and which allows them to analyse all the activities on different sites and social networks.

Most of these sites give you detailed information about your digital identity, visibility score (with a maximum precision) and e-reputation.

At the latter level, they manage to analyse the reactions of Internet users and determine whether these reactions are positive or negative towards you. They therefore often use very sophisticated tools at the level of analysis and often call upon Artificial Intelligence.

These analyses allow you to have a fairly accurate view of your online reputation and to take the necessary actions to improve your online reputation.

<u>The most popular are:</u>

- Mention (www.mention.com/en/)
- Réputations VIP (www.reputationvip.com/en/)
- Synthesio (www.synthesio.com)
- Linkfluence (www.linkfluence.com)
- Trackur (www.trackur.com)
- Buzzsumo (www.buzzsumo.com)
- Sprinklr (www.sprinklr.com)
- Buzzstream (www.buzzstream.com)

A vous de faire votre choix entre ces différents outils en fonction de votre budget et de vos besoins.

The American case

A small remark about the United States, which also offers information services on a person, but with a slightly different approach, since it verifies whether that person has a good reputation in the very broad sense of the term.

The analysis is not only done on social networks, but it also tells you whether the person has been convicted, deported, or subjected to any other legal measures that may harm the person's reputation. Some even call upon the denunciation of Internet users.

It is clear that this kind of practice is not possible in our country and it is certainly a good thing.

Because even if the practice is legal, since these sites are based on information that has been published and more or less publicly accessible, the invasion of privacy and respect for the individual seems somewhat forgotten to me. How do you feel about that?

Step 2: Correct what can be rectified!

The Internet does not forget anything!

It is important to be aware of one thing: everything we publish on the Internet leaves an indelible mark that can be used against us by companies or individuals.
We were able to judge it in the previous stage.
For example, some people have even been dismissed for statements made against their employers on their Facebook walls.

Be aware that some of the traces we have left on the Internet seem to be forgotten. But know that some sites, such as Facebook or Google, keep all information about us even if it has been deleted or seems to have been forgotten.

Google under pressure from the EEC

When traces damage your reputation, you can try to have them erased.

Google, for example, provides you with a "search result deletion request under European data protection legislation" (good!). However, according to the latest figures available, 70% of applications are refused.

To increase your chances to the maximum, I suggest that you use a specialised site such as www.forget.me, which is currently free of charge.

Privatise to a maximum

At the level of your contacts, it is important to separate private and professional life.

There are 2 solutions.

The first, the most radical, is to have 2 accounts on each social network.
A personal account with a detailed profile, a nickname (or a name like "Pierre C") and welcoming your friends and family. A professional with a light profile, with your full name and intended for your professional contacts. This is the most efficient, but it is difficult to set up if you already have a well-developed account.

Alternatively, limit your information to your main account and classify your "friends" in different categories (friends, family, colleagues, customers, suppliers, etc.) or at least two (private & professional). In this way, when you publish something, you can choose to whom it is meant for.
You will thus be able to privatise certain contents in the sight of recruiters (holiday photos, evening photos...). This allows you not to give a picture of yourself that you do not want to give.

Be vigilant on the contacts met briefly (at parties or events) and with the "old" people (colleagues, classmates, etc.), in this shadowy area may hide some unpleasant surprises...
It is difficult to see how much personal information is available to naughty people.

All responsible!

Importantly, without being self-righteous, keep a close watch on what you publish and think about the professional repercussions this could have now or in the future!
Basic principle:"better safe than sorry!"

You can only find on the Internet what Internet users have agreed to leave behind.
With regard to your personal information, it is rare for a person to deliberately insist on having your personal data disseminated without your consent.

The best way to avoid any problems is not to publish them yourself.
Don't you want your age to be available? Do not give your date of birth.
Afraid of misconceiving your photo albums? Do not post your photos on Facebook, send them by email or via a site that respects your privacy.

Behave as if all shared content online could become public. Because the rules of a social network can change abruptly or there can be a bug (which happened several times on Facebook, revealing information that was supposed to remain confidential) or your "friends" can publicly share content that you published under "private"status.

And in any case, avoid greedy tweets and its painful awakenings or posts criticising your company (or applaud a competitor) and its inevitable consequences...

Remove the superfluous

Delete outdated or unnecessary information (old photos, traces of watered-out exits, etc.).

Also, delete social networks that you have signed up for but never visit. If it seems complicated to you, a site like www.justdelete.me can help you by telling you, for each site, how to proceed.

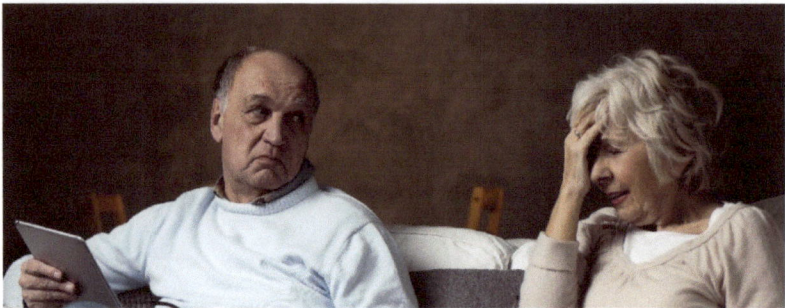

The danger of "... for free"

A well-known marketing principle says:"If it's free, it's YOU the product!".
This rage of Internet users to favour free services forgets that nothing is free and that someone has to pay for local, personal and IT costs.
So "free"services, most of the time, use your data or sell them to the highest bidder.
Isn't that more expensive than a paid service?
So don't sacrifice "respect for your privacy" to have a "digital identity"...

Step 3: Refine your professional identity!

It is important to have maximum visibility.
But you must not disperse.
Loss of time = loss of efficiency.

If you only need to focus on two social networks, I advise you:
if you work in a B2C company: LinkedIn + Twitter
if you work in a B2B company: LinkedIn + Facebook
if you work in fashion, graphics or decoration: LinkedIn + Instagram
etc.

How to choose?
Find out where your professional entourage, interlocutors, customers and potential customers are active.
And choose the MOST RELEVANT PLACES TO BE!

Optimise your LinkedIn profile

As you will have noticed in the examples above, I systematically advise you to include LinkedIn in the social networks you choose to develop.

Why? Why? Because LinkedIn is THE professional reference and a guarantee of seriousness.

In addition, the user community guarantees maximum professional visibility.

Finally, it is the favourite place of headhunters...

On the other hand, LinkedIn asks that your profile be up to date and highlight your skills.

Here are some tips:

Professional photography is essential

In order to be recognised by your contacts and identifiable by others, a professional photo must be included in your LinkedIn profile. Avoid selfies, photos taken with a webcam and cropped holiday photos! Be professional, have a portrait made by a professional or a particularly gifted relative. Remember also to show yourself in your best light...

Integrate a banner

LinkedIn proposes to integrate a banner in the background on the same principle as the "cover" Twitter and Facebook. The recommended size is 1400x425px. The background is used to highlight your profile. You can do this easily via free graphic design sites such as www.canva.com.

Write a presentation

The first thing a visitor will read on your profile is the "Summary" area at the top of the profile. It should contain a summary of your professional profile, experiences and values. It must also reflect your situation on the job market: in standby, in post, in active search... Put yourself forward, be a salesman, but without being heavy.
Be concise, remember that short texts are more readable.

Detail your "feats"

The skill section is obviously very important.
So take the time, company by company, to detail your positions, missions, projects on which you worked, but also especially what you got out of it.
Your interlocutors will often be curious to know what you have learned from your different experiences and how it has nourished you.
If you have been successful, say so! increase in turnover, successful projects, etc.

Focus your profile on your goal
Needless to say, you have been a supermarket salesman or summer camp instructor if you do not intend to continue in this direction.
Focus your profile and detail the experiences that are related to your career goals.

Share content
LinkedIn is a social network like any other social network except that it is reserved for professionals and professional considerations. Don't post your holiday photos! There are other networks for that. On the other hand, share your professional experience, your watch, and any content that can be a proof of your professional knowledge and know-how.

Show your expertise in Groups
LinkedIn groups allow you to get in touch and collect intelligence in each sector. Some target groups are more interesting than others in your field, find them and sign up! They are frequented by many players in the sector (and by recruiters). It's the perfect place to get noticed by posting, or taking part in discussions. Analyze how the best people behave and imitate them.

Recommend, be recommended!
Recommendations, even if they are of relative value, can nevertheless enhance your experience and skills. Recommend your friends, colleagues, former colleagues, etc. LinkedIn will suggest them to do the same for you.
This will help to feed your e-reputation in addition to other actions.

Be subtle!
LinkedIn is not a sales site. It's important to showcase yourself, but in a subtle way. Your network is built over time, feed it and enrich it regularly. The size of your network will also contribute

to your e-reputation. Your digital identity will be well insured by LinkedIn, if you only have to be present and active on ONE social network, professionally, it is this one!

Be effective on other social networks

As we have just seen, LinkedIn is a professional social network that cannot be ignored for your digital identity.

If you really want to get visibility, I advise you to be active on, at a minimum, another social network. Choose it according to your industry and the type of content you want to share (Instagram or Pinterest for graphics, YouTube for video, etc.).

The two general social networks are Facebook and Twitter. I personally have a preference for Twitter, but ask where your potential interlocutors are active, this is where you should be!

Some valuable tips on most social networks

A real activity
To build your e-reputation, build and develop your network, you need to be active and post regularly. It is essential to feed your community with content. It does not necessarily have to be produced by you. You can easily share other people's content, from your social network or readings on certain sites or information feeds.
An account that does not regularly post is not the best effect, image matter, and will not be "tracked"anyway.

"Follow" to be "followed"
You must search for and follow other profiles in your business area. First choose the most active accounts with a large number of followers.
This will allow you, on the one hand, to collect topics that you can share with your own community. And, on the other hand, to have the chance to be followed by the owner of this account yourself and to be noticed by your publications.

Expand your Branding
Like LinkedIn, insert a nice photo (or logo, if you have one) and a cover banner on your account. It is important to attract as much attention as possible.

Everything must point to your site
Include a link to your corporate website for those who want to know more about you.
If you don't have a website, you can put the URL of your LinkedIn account or create a presentation page on a website like www.about.be.
If you have a site, on the one hand, write the content and publish the link to it.

On the other hand, make a link in the other direction between your site and this social network in order to make your visitors followers.

Mention your social networks in all your communication
In your online communication, but also "paper", as well as in your e-mail signature, indicate a link to the social networks in which you are actually active.

If you don't have the time
Or, designate an employee to search for information to post or share.
Or contact a specialised agency.

Step 4: Exist digitally!

To exist digitally on social networks is to share content.

You have two types of content:
On the one hand, the one you find and which seems important to you. If you share it on social networks, you become a "smuggler". There is no shame in that, excellent smugglers who do a very good watch and post only the best content for their community, are followed by tens of thousands of Internet users.

On the other hand, the one you produce will be relayed by others, the "couriers".

Producing content may not seem natural to you.
I'll try to recommend the easiest way.

On what subject?

The easiest way is to start with the three components of your professional identity:

- functions/jobs
- knowledge/competence/expertise
- human qualities/values

To make it simple, write down what you are passionate about and what you benefit from the best know-how.

Do you have an "editorial strategy"?

For your personal digital identity to be effective, it must be accurate.

No matter if you are a specialist or a general practitioner, it is irrelevant to communicate about everything you know how to do!

You need to define a competency axis.

To put it bluntly, many people need to "label" the people they meet/read. If they say to each other about you:"I don't know exactly what that person is doing", your digital identity will take a hit!

Therefore, your editorial line must be clear and precise. Your network must be able to identify you on ONE subject (which can, of course, be broken down into subtopics).

And if you have multiple talents

You can also create a blog on one topic and another on another. This will interest two different audiences.

Still to think about: a blog is hard to manage... two blogs, it's...?

Sometimes, you have to choose and choose is to know how to give up!

First of all...

Step 5: Get under control!

It is important not to sail in fog!
If you have decided to devote time to developing your digital identity, give yourself the time and/or means to make it as productive as possible.

Choose a monitoring service

You need to have an overview of the efforts and, above all, the results achieved.
In addition, you control your digital identity (what we know about you), you must have the most accurate view possible of your e-reputation (what we say about you).

Subscribe to one of the main e-reputation sites:
- Mention (www.mention.com)
- Réputations VIP (www.reputationvip.com)
- Synthesio (www.synthesio.com)
- Linkfluence (www.linkfluence.com)
- Trackur (www.trackur.com)
- Buzzsumo (www.buzzsumo.com)
- Sprinklr (www.sprinklr.com)
- Buzzstream (www.buzzstream.com)

All of these sites charge a fee, but most offer a free trial period. Choose the one that fits your budget and provides the data you need.

⁇

Alert services

There are also alert services that will let you know when someone mentions your name or brand/company. Be careful, these services do not give you any monitoring of social networks.

The best known warning system is Google Alerts (www.google.fr/alerts).

Its operation is very simple, you determine what you want the alert to be made on a person's name or company name or other criteria and the site creates an alert. The site will search regularly in the different sites, blocks and social networks where the search you have defined can appear. And you will be notified on a regular basis, either daily or weekly, of the results of this monitoring.

Another site that can offer a good alternative to Google alerts is Talkwalker (https://www.talkwalker.com/alerts) which offers exactly the same features. It's up to you to test both formulas and choose the one you like best.

de | en | fr

talkwalkeralerts   CRÉER   â Se connecter

Créer une alerte

RECHERCHE	
RÉSULTATS	Tout
LANGUE	Toutes les langues
FRÉQUENCE	Une fois par jour
VOLUME	Seulement les meilleurs résultats
VOTRE EMAIL	

☐ I have read and agree to the Terms and Conditions

🔍 Aperçu   CRÉER l'alerte

Talkwalker Alertes - la meilleure alternative à Google Alertes, simple et gratuite

Surveillez votre e-réputation, celle d'une marque, d'un concurrent, d'un événement ou du dernier buzz qui a marqué le Web !

Talkwalker Alertes est un moyen simple et gratuit de surveiller n'importe quel sujet sur le web. Il vous permet de recevoir par email ou de lire via un lecteur de flux RSS, les derniers résultats publiés sur le web.

Talkwalker.com | Support / Commentaires | Syntaxe de recherche | Conditions d'utilisation | Kit Presse

Keep your site under surveillance

If you have a site, install Google Analytics.
It will give you accurate traffic data from social networks.

Define objectives

Set yourself specific goals (for example: earn x points on the Klout score or increase my community of x Twitter subscribers or have x new contacts in my area on LinkedIn), measurable and achievable.
This is the best way to find out if your work has paid off or if you need to redouble your efforts.

Protect your social networks from the inevitable

On social networks, managing accounts after death is a sensitive issue.

On Google, you just have to go to the settings of your profile to plan the deletion of your account after your death.

On Facebook, relatives of deceased people can already transform a deceased person's account into a "memorial profile": some elements are hidden in order to respect the deceased person's privacy and the groups to which he or she belonged are automatically removed. But many Internet users tell me that this is not an easy thing. Other measures have been put in place but do not appear to be perfect.

The easiest way is to put your identifiers (or the place where they are) in your will. The notary or someone close to you will then be responsible for closing all your accounts.
Yes, digital identity has an end...   🙂

In summary

Digital identity, a necessity for everyone!

At a time when everything is going online and everyone can learn about everyone, it is essential to master their digital identity.

Whether you are an employee, a job seeker, a manager, a self-employed person or a professional, you must offer the best possible image of yourself!

And remember, digital identity theft does exist!

So avoid, by negligence, being a victim or simply being ignored by your professional entourage...

E-reputation is not reserved for an elite

If you are active on the Internet and, in specific, on social networks, you are able to make comments that I hope will be positive.

The way we see and appreciate you will build your e-reputation. It's worth it, because this one can bring you a promotion, new customers and, in any case, consideration around you!

Be careful!

Don't ever post anything you don't want everyone to have access to it, and always think about the fact that we're all under surveillance, one way or another...

If you want very personal considerations or confidential information, use other communication channels than social networks.

⍰

Be professional!

If you really want to improve your digital identity and develop your e-reputation, give yourself the means and devote time to it. Follow the various tips of this book which was intended to be a practical work and accessible to all.

Sources

Gallup:
http://products.gallup.com/171722/state-american-consumer.aspx
Norton:
http://now.symassets.com/now/fr/pu/images/Promotions/2016/PDFs/Norton%20Online%20Reputation%20Report%20-%20FR.pdf

A big thank you!

This book has been translated from French to English by Deepl.
www.DeepL.com/Translator

If you discover any errors or if you have any comments, please do not hesitate to contact me at www.pierrecat.com.

Follow me! Follow me!

Web : www.pierrecat.com

LinkedIn : www.linkedin.com/in/pierrecat/

Twitter : www.twitter.com/pierre_cat

YouTube : www.youtube.com/channel/

Google+ : plus.google.com/u/0/+PierreCat

Instagram : www.instagram.com/pierre.cat.consulting/

Pinterest : www.pinterest.fr/pierrecatconsulting/

Facebook : www.facebook.com/pierre.cat.consulting/